The First Light

The Greatest Prophet ﷺ

Āyatullāh Ḥusayn
Waḥīd Khurāsānī

AL-BURĀQ

Copyright

ISBN: 978-1-956276-29-9

Printed and published by al-Burāq Publications.

Translated and annotated by al-Burāq Publications. Where needed, context and transliterations were added. Some minor edits were made to the translated Arabic text.

Ordering Information
We offer discounts and promotions for wholesale purchases, non-profit organizations, and other educational institutions. Contact us at the email below for further information.

www.al-Buraq.org
publications@al-Buraq.org

First Edition | January 2023

Dedication

The publication of this book was made possible through the generous support of our donors.

Please recite *Sūrat al-Fātiha* and ask God for the Divine reward (*thawāb*) to be conferred upon the donors and also the souls of all the deceased in whose memory their loved ones have contributed graciously towards the publication of *The First Light: The Greatest Prophet (s).*

We begin by giving all praise and thanks to God for giving us the tawfiq to translate this book. He has guided us and without Him, we would not have been guided to the straight path embodied by the Prophet Muḥammad and the Ahl al-Bayt.

This book is dedicated firstly to Āyatullāh Ḥusayn Waḥīd Khurāsānī, who made tremendous strides in advancing the cause of Islam. It is also dedicated to all the scholars, martyrs and believers who worked tirelessly to promote the pure Muḥammadan path.

We want to also give our thanks and appreciation to all believers from around the world and acknowledge the team which helped al-Burāq Publications complete this work, spending countless hours to make its publication possible. Please recite Sūrat al-Fātiḥah on behalf of them, their families, and their marḥūmīn.

This book is dedicated in honor of the following individuals. Please remember them in your prayers and may God have mercy on them and their loved ones.

Abbas Alihussain

Abdul Ali Sheikh

Abduladheem Muhaimeed

Agha A. Hussain

Akhter Moosavi

Ali Al Barak

Ali Ftouni

Alya Agemy

Amir Moledina

Anwarali Khimji

Azim Panju

Bande Khuda

Fatima Kaneez

Fatima N. Hasan

Fidahussein J. Moledina

Haji Abdi Mourad

Haji Mofida Fadel

Haji Sobhie Saab

Haji Zahra Ghacham

Hajj Ahmed Koussan

Hajj Ghacham Ghacham

Hajj Hassan Sobh

Hajj Mahmoud Mazeh

Hajj Sami Ftouni

Hajj Youssef Chahine

Hajji Amneh Sobh-Ftouni

Mirza Mazher A. Baig

MohammadAli Naquvi

Mohammed Zuhair

Mohammedali Alidina

Mohsin Jafri

Mona Manoun

Mujtaba Rizvi

Munawwar Jehan

Musharaf Fatima

Nafees Khan

Naji Mujahid

Naqi H. Abedi

Noorimabai Banatwala

Rajabali Damani

Rameez Mehdi

Razia Sarfaraz

Rubab Alidina

Sabiha N. H. Jafri

Sayed AliHaider

Sayeda Asghari A. Ara

Sayyid Sobh H. Sobh

Shaheed Ibrahim Hadi

Shandar Fatima

Sugra Khimji

Syed Fidvi Ali

Syed Mehdi Ahmed

Hajji Hiam Hojeije
Hajji Imane Srour
Hajji Zeinab Anani
Hani Yehia
Hayder Aljabury
Heba Allouche
Hussain Shaheedi
Ibrahim Yassin
Imaan Husain
Jenan Abaid
Kadhum Shakarchi
Khadije Sarhan
Khatoonbhai Moledina
Khursheed R. Najafi
Kulsumbhai Damani
Layla Yaghi
Mahmoud Tiba
Malika Begum
Mariam Al Haj Hussein
Mehrunnisa Jafri
Mirza Ahmed A. Baig
Syed Mehdi H. Rizvi
Syed Mujtaba Ahmed
Syed Mustafa Moosvi
Syed Nawab R. Kazmi
Syed Nurul H. Jafri
Syed Yousuf Hussain
Syeda Amina Begum
Syeda Batool
Syeda Majeeda
Syeda Masooma Begum
Syeda Waheeda
Taqia Naqvi
Tasleem Fatima
Tilmiz H. Rizvi
Turfah Sobh
Yasmeen A. Banatwala
Zahra A. Hasan
Zainab Qasimhasan
Zakiya Begum
Zaynab M. Hasan
Zaynab Todd

Duʿāʾ al-Ḥujjah

اللَّهُمَّ كُنْ لِوَلِيِّكَ الْحُجَّةِ بْنِ الْحَسَنِ صَلَوَاتُكَ
عَلَيْهِ وَعَلَى آبَائِهِ فِي هَذِهِ السَّاعَةِ وَفِي كُلِّ
سَاعَةٍ وَلِيّاً وَحَافِظاً وَقَائِداً وَنَاصِراً وَدَلِيلاً
وَعَيْناً حَتَّى تُسْكِنَهُ أَرْضَكَ طَوْعاً وَتُمَتِّعَهُ فِيهَا طَوِيلاً

O God, be, for Your representative, the Ḥujjat (proof), son of al-Ḥasan, Your blessings be upon him and his forefathers, in this hour and in every hour: a guardian, a protector, a leader, a helper, a proof, and an eye - until You make him live on the Earth, in obedience (to You), and cause him to live in it for a long time.

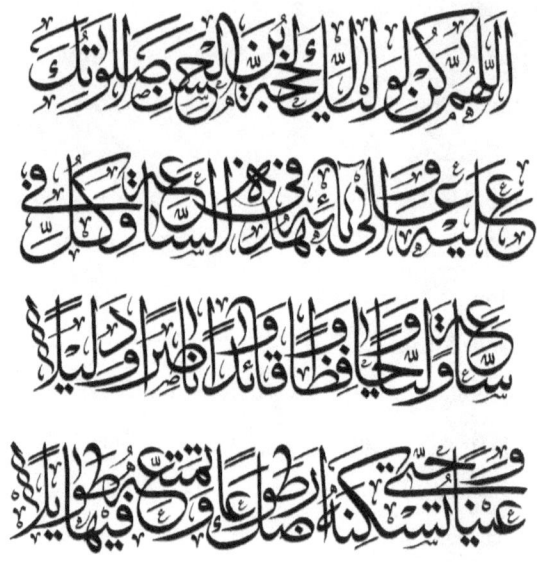

Terms of Respect

The following Arabic phrases have been used throughout this book in their respective places to show the reverence which the noble personalities deserve.

عزّ وجلّ
Used for God, meaning:
Exalted and Sublime (Perfect) is He

صلى الله عليه وآله
Used for Prophet Muḥammad, meaning:
Blessings from God be upon him and his family

عليه السلام
Used for a man (singular) of a high status, meaning:
Peace be upon him

عليها السلام
Used for a woman (singular) of a high status, meaning:
Peace be upon her

عليهما السلام
Used for men/women (dual) of a high status, meaning:
Peace be upon them both

عليهم السلام
Used for men and/or women (plural) of a high status, meaning:
Peace be upon them all

عجّل الله تعالى فرجه الشريف
Used for Imām Muḥammad al-Mahdī, meaning:
May God hasten his return

قدّس سرّه
Used for a deceased scholar, meaning:
May his resting [burial] place remain pure

Transliteration Table

The method of transliteration of Islamic terminology from the Arabic language has been carried out according to the standard transliteration table below.

ء	ʾ	ر	r	ف	f
ا	a	ز	z	ق	q
ب	b	س	s	ك	k
ت	t	ش	sh	ل	l
ث	th	ص	ṣ	م	m
ج	j	ض	ḍ	ن	n
ح	ḥ	ط	ṭ	و	w
خ	kh	ظ	ẓ	هـ	h
د	d	ع	ʿ	ي	y
ذ	dh	غ	gh		
Long Vowels					
ا	ā	و	ū	ي	ī
Short Vowels					
ـَ	a	ـُ	u	ـِ	i

Table of Contents

Introduction

بسم الله الرحمن الرحيم

In the Name of God, the Beneficent, the Merciful

Peace and blessings be upon the noblest Prophet and Messenger, our Master Muḥammad and his immaculate household and eternal curses be upon their enemies.

It is difficult for an ordinary person who is not connected to the heavens to realize the reality of those who are connected to the heavens, metaphysical dimensions and the Creator of the universe! How, then, can he realize the reality of the first human being in the world of existence, the perfect individual amongst creation, the last of those who preceded him and the conqueror of what is yet to come?

There is no doubt that by making this attempt, he would be aiming at the stars in the sky, while resting his feet on earth. This resonates with the poet's saying:

It's the sun whose home is in the sky; so, console the heart with beautiful consolation.

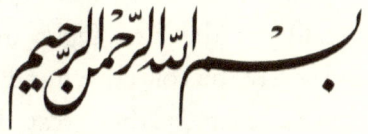

This is our state, where we aim at getting to know the reality of the First Light and most perfect mind – nay the collective mind and the complete mind that is the great Prophet Muḥammad b. ʿAbdillāh ﷺ. Nonetheless, we have resources such as the Noble Qur'ān, the Prophetic aḥadīth and the words of the immaculate Imāms عليهم السلام that can enlighten us with the knowledge that our human capacity can endure.

Surely, we – as individuals – feel intimidated from entering that world and roaming that ocean, let alone diving into it. For this purpose, we need someone to hold our hands and introduce us to the clear and straight path, lest we enter a labyrinth from which we cannot escape. That's why we have chosen for you, dear readers, and on the occasion of the martyrdom of the First and Greatest Light ﷺ, this booklet extracted from the book "*Muqaḍḍima 'ila 'Usūl al-Dīn*" by the great Āyatullāh Ḥusayn Waḥīd Khurāsānī.

And God is the one who guides and bestows success and victory. Praise be to God, first and lastly.

Dar al-Siddiqa al-Shahida

30 Muharram, 1431 AH

The Blessed Messenger Muḥammad ﷺ

بسم الله الرحمن الرحيم

In the Name of God, the Beneficent, the Merciful

Peace and blessings be upon our Master Muḥammad and his immaculate household ﷺ, especially the Remnant of God in the Worlds عجل الله تعالى فرجه الشريف.

His Birth ﷺ

He was born on the 17th of Rabīʿ al-Awwal according to the popular opinion of the elites, and on the 12th of Rabīʿ al-Awwal based on the general popular opinion.

His Names ﷺ

Some of his names are: Muḥammad, Aḥmad, ʿAbdullāh, Yā-Sīn, Nūn, Ṭā Ḥā, al-Fātiḥ (The Conqueror), al-Khātam (The Last), al-Kāf, al-Muqaffa and al-Ḥashir (The Gatherer).

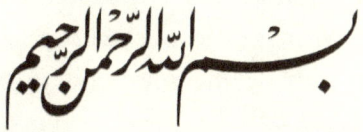

His Attributes ﷺ

Some of the attributes given to him by God ﷻ were: the witness, the one who passes good news, the warner, the one who calls people towards God ﷻ upon His permission, the enlightening lantern and the Last Prophet.

His Titles ﷺ

Some of the titles through which God ﷻ addressed him were: O' Prophet, O' Messenger, O' Enwrapped One, O' Shrouded.

His Nicknames ﷺ

Some of his nicknames were: Abū al-Qāsim, Abū al-Ṭāhir, Abū al-Ṭayyib, Abū al-Masākīn (father of the poor and vulnerable), Abū al-Durratayn (father of the two gems), Abū al-Rayḥānatayn (father of the two basil flowers) and Abū al-Ṣibṭayn (father of the two maternal grandsons).

His Virtues ﷺ

His ﷺ virtues are too numerous to be stated on these papers and too great to be comprehended; for, how can one comprehend the virtues of the one who is the Beloved of the Lord of all Worlds ﷻ, the best of all creations, the last Prophet and Master of all messengers, the leader of the guided and guiding Imāms ﵈, the one who God addressed as Ṭā Ḥā and Yā-Sīn, and the first worshiper from amongst the first and last people due to his approval by saying "yes"[1]

---

[1] This is in reference to the noble verse:

﴿وَإِذْ أَخَذَ رَبُّكَ مِن بَنِي آدَمَ مِن ظُهُورِهِمْ ذُرِّيَّتَهُمْ وَأَشْهَدَهُمْ عَلَىٰ أَنفُسِهِمْ أَلَسْتُ بِرَبِّكُمْ قَالُوا بَلَىٰ شَهِدْنَا﴾

﴾wa-'idh 'akhadha rabbuka min banī 'ādama min ẓuhūrihim dhurriyyatahum wa-'ashhadahum 'alā 'anfusihim 'a-lastu bi-rabbikum qālū balā shahidnā﴿

﴾When your Lord took from the Children of Adam, from their loins, their descendants and made them bear witness over themselves, [He said to them,] 'Am I not your Lord?' They said, 'Yes indeed! We bear witness.'﴿

Sūrat al-A'rāf, Verse 172.

when the pledge was taken regarding the lordship of God ﷻ, the Lord of all Worlds.

In a word, he is the Great Name of God and the ideal manifestation of God, the King, the Righteous and the Manifest.

We can only admit to our incapacity and shortcomings in identifying the attributes of the one who God ﷻ described as the witness, the one who gives good news, the warner, the one who calls people towards God ﷻ with His ﷻ permission and the enlightening lantern. Nonetheless, we will mention some of which He ﷻ imparted on the Prophet's nation in honor of him ﷺ, in addition to the verse with which God ﷻ blessed us:

﴿لَّقَدْ كَانَ لَكُمْ فِي رَسُولِ اللَّهِ أُسْوَةٌ حَسَنَةٌ
لِّمَن كَانَ يَرْجُو اللَّهَ وَالْيَوْمَ الْآخِرَ وَذَكَرَ اللَّهَ كَثِيرًا﴾

﴿la-qad kāna lakum fī rasūli llāhi ʾuswatun ḥasanatun li-man kāna yarjū llāha wa-l-yawma l-ʾākhira wa-dhakara llāha kathīra^{n}﴾

﴾*In the Apostle of God there is certainly for you a good exemplar, for those who look forward to God and the Last Day, and remember God greatly*﴿[2]

It is narrated that Bakr b. ʿAbdillāh said that ʿUmar b. al-Khaṭṭāb entered the room, and the Prophet ﷺ was feverish, so ʿUmar said to him, "O' Messenger of God, your fever is so severe!" He ﷺ said, "This didn't keep me from reading thirty Surahs – of which seven are long." ʿUmar, then, said, "O' Messenger of God, may God forgive all your past and future sins given all your hard work and efforts." He ﷺ said, "O' ʿUmar, shouldn't I be a grateful servant!"[3]

This excludes his mandatory prayers every night, whereby he worshiped his Lord until his legs and feet were swollen.

---

[2] Sūrat al-Aḥzāb, Verse 21.

[3] Ṭūsī, Shaykh Muḥammad b. Ḥasan, *al-Amālī*, p. 403.

In this regard[4], God ﷻ sent the following verse:

﴿طه﴾

﴿*Ṭā Ḥā*﴾

﴿مَا أَنْزَلْنَا عَلَيْكَ الْقُرْآنَ لِتَشْقَىٰ﴾

﴿*mā ʾanzalnā ʿalayka l-qurʾāna li-tashqā*﴾

﴿*Ṭā Hā! We did not send down to* you *the Qurʾān that* you *should be miserable*﴾[5]

It is narrated that Jābir b. ʿAbdillāh said, "The Messenger of God was never asked for anything to which he responded with rejection."[6]

It is narrated that Imām ʿAlī b. Abī Ṭālib, Amīr al-Muʾminīn ؑ said, "He was the most generous of people, had the boldest heart and most honest tongue; he was the most loyal, the

[4] Review al-Ṭabrisī, Shaykh Aḥmad b. ʿAlī, *al-Ihtijaj,* Vol. 1, p. 326.

[5] Sūrat Ṭā Ḥā, Verses 1-2.

[6] Ṭabrisī, Shaykh Faḍl b. Ḥasan, *Makārim al-Akhlāq*, p. 18.

most lenient and the kindest in dealing with others. He who first sees him, feels intimated; and he who spends time with him and gets to know him, loves him. I have never seen anyone —before or after him—like him."[7]

It is also narrated that 'Amīr al-Mu'minīn ؑ said, "When the war would get severe and the two armies face one another, we would shield ourselves by the Messenger of God; for, no one would be closer to the enemy than him."[8]

He was known amongst his enemies by his trustworthiness, such that his popular name amongst them was al-'Amīn (the trustworthy).

He was known by them as an honest man. Even Abū Jahl said, "We do not claim you to be a liar; however, we deny what you brought us."[9]

---

[7] Ibid. p. 17.

[8] Ibid. p. 18.

[9] Ṭabrisī, Shaykh Faḍl b. Ḥasan, *Majma' al-Bayān fī Tafsīr al-Qur'ān*, Vol. 4, p. 42.

Thus, the following verse descended:

﴿فَإِنَّهُمْ لَا يُكَذِّبُونَكَ﴾

﴿*fa-'innahum lā yukadhdhibūnaka*﴾

﴿*Yet, it is not* you *that they deny*﴾[10]

His gatherings were that of knowledge, tolerance, modesty and dignity.[11]

His knees would never get ahead of his companion's.[12] He used to lower his gaze and often looked at the ground more than the skies.[13]

He was mostly quiet; as he didn't speak except when needed. He used to turn away from those who spoke of indecent matters.[14]

---

[10] Sūrat al-An'ām, Verse 33

[11] Ṭabrisī, Shaykh Faḍl b. Ḥasan, *Makārim al-Akhlāq*, p. 14.

[12] Ibid. p. 17.

[13] Ṣadūq, Shaykh Muḥammad b. 'Alī, *'Uyūn Akhbār al-Riḍā*, Ch. 29, ḥadīth 1, p. 317.

[14] Ṭabrisī, Shaykh Faḍl b. Ḥasan, *Makārim al-Akhlāq*, p. 13.

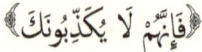

His laughter was expressed through smiling[15] and his speech was decisive[16]. He would only speak righteously, regardless of whether he is in a state of contentment or anger.[17]

He would neither sit down nor stand up except in remembrance of God ﷻ.[18]

If a person joins his company and sits beside him, he would not stand up except after this person stands.[19]

In the authenticated book of narrations by Jamīl b. Darrāj, it is narrated that Abā Abdillāh ؑ said, "The Messenger of God used to divide his time amongst his companions equally. He would look at this person or that in the same way." He said: "The Messenger of God never stretched his legs in front of his companions.

---

15 Ibid.

16 Ibid. p. 23.

17 Ibn al-Maghāzlī, *Manāqīb al-Imām ʿAlī b. Abī Tālib*, Vol. 1, p. 147.

18 Ṭabrisī, Shaykh Faḍl b. Ḥasan, *Makārim al-Akhlāq*, p. 14.

19 Ibid.

And when a man shook his hand, the Messenger of God would not let go of his hand until that person removed his hand first."[20]

Once, he was traveling; so he ordered one of his companions to slaughter a sheep. One of the men rose and said, "O' Messenger of God, I will be the one who slaughters the sheep." Another man said, "And I will skin it." Another man said, "And I will cut it." Then another man said, "And I will cook it." The Messenger of God, then, said, "I need to gather some firewood for you." So, they said to him, "O' Messenger of God, do not exhaust yourself. May we sacrifice our fathers and mothers for you! We will suffice you." He said, "I know that you would suffice me. However, God hates to see a person singled out from amongst his companions." And so, he

[20] Kulaynī, Shaykh Muḥammad b. Yaʿqūb, *al-Kāfī*, Vol. 2, p. 671.

got up and set off to collect some firewood for them.[21]

It is narrated that ʾAnas b. Mālik said, "The Messenger of God used to break his fast with a sip of water and would then take a sip of water as his pre-dawn meal. And perhaps it was only one sip. And perhaps it was yogurt. And perhaps it was soaked bread which I prepared for him one night, but the Prophet abstained from it. So, I thought that he had been invited over for dinner by one of his companions so I drank it myself. Then he came back one hour past dinner time. I asked some of his companions whether the Prophet had had dinner or been invited by anyone, to which they responded with rejection.

I spent that night with extreme fear of encountering the situation where the Prophet would come and ask me for it, then wouldn't find it and sleep through the night on an empty

---

[21] Ṭabrisī, Shaykh Faḍl b. Ḥasan, *Makārim al-Akhlāq*, p. 252.

al-Shāmī, Shaykh Muḥammad b. Yūsuf al-Ṣāliḥī, *Subul al-Hudā wal Rashād fi Sīrat Khayr al-ʿIbād*, Vol. 7, p. 13.

stomach. However, he woke up in a fasting state and didn't ask me about it or mention it until this very day."[22]

It was also narrated by him that the Prophet ﷺ encountered an Arabian man who took him tightly by his garment and pulled him close to him until his neck was affected by the firmness of his pull, then he said to the Prophet ﷺ, "O' Muḥammad, give the order upon which I am granted some of the money which God has entrusted to you." The Messenger of God ﷺ looked at him, laughed and gave the order of provision.[23]

It has been mentioned in al-Ṣaḥīḥ that Imām Muḥammad al-Bāqir ؑ said, "A Jew came to the Messenger of God while 'Ā'isha was with him. He said, "May death be sent upon you." The Messenger of God said, "And you." Then, another one came in and said the same thing, to which the Prophet gave the same response. Then another came in and said the same thing, and the Messenger of God responded similarly.

---

22 Ṭabrisī, Shaykh Faḍl b. Ḥasan, *Makārim al-Akhlāq*, p. 32.

23 Ibid., p. 17.

ʿĀʾisha, then, got angry and said, "May death, anger and curses be sent upon you, O' Jewish people, O' brothers of monkeys and pigs." Thus, the Messenger of God said to her, "O' ʿĀʾisha, had obscenity been exemplified by anything, it would have been a bad example. Meanwhile, whenever kindness touches a thing it beautifies it, and whenever it leaves a thing it dishonors it..."[24]

It has also been mentioned in *al-Ṣaḥīḥ* by Abān al-Aḥmar, that Imām Jaʿfar al-Ṣādiq ؑ said, "A man came to the Messenger of God whose clothes were shabby. So, he gave him twelve Dirhams and said, "O' ʿAlī, take these Dirhams and buy me a garment I can wear." ʿAlī said, "I went to the market and bought him a garment for twelve Dirhams. I took it to the Messenger of God who looked at it and said, "O' ʿAlī, I would have loved another option better, do you think its owner would take it back?" I said:, "I don't know." He said, "Check with him." So I went to the owner and said, "The Messenger of God didn't like this garment and wanted something of less value and cost. So, kindly

---

[24] Kulaynī, Shaykh Muḥammad b. Yaʿqūb, *al-Kāfī*, Vol. 2, p. 648.

spare us and take it back." Thus, the owner gave me back the Dirhams which I brought to the Messenger of God. He came with me to the market to buy a garment, when he saw a bond-maid sitting and crying on the street. So, the Messenger of God asked her, "What is the matter?" She said, "O' Messenger of God, my family gave me four Dirhams to buy an item, but they were lost and I cannot go back to them empty-handed." Thus, the Messenger of God gave her four Dirhams and said, "Go back to your family."

Then, the Messenger of God continued his journey to the market and bought a garment for four Dirhams, wore it and praised God. On his way out, he saw a naked man saying, "Whoever clothes me, may God cover him with the clothes of Heaven!"

Thereupon, the Messenger of God took off his garment which he had just bought and covered the man's shoulders with it. Then, he went back to the market and bought another garment with the four Dirhams left. He wore it and praised God. Then, on his way back home, he saw the bond-maid sitting on the street, so he asked her, "Why haven't you returned to your family yet?"

She said, "It's been a long time since I left home and I fear they will beat me when I go back." So, the Messenger of God said, "Walk in front of me and lead me to your family." Thus, the Messenger of God arrived and stood at their door, then he said, "Peace be upon you, O' people of this home." However, they didn't respond. So, he sent his peace upon them again, yet they didn't respond.

Then, he repeated his greetings, upon which they said, "Peace and blessings be upon you, O' Messenger of God." So, he said to them, "How come you didn't respond to me the first two times? They said: O' Messenger of God, we heard your greetings; and so, we loved to hear more of it."

Then, the Messenger of God said, "This bond-maid has run a bit late, do not punish her." They said, "O' Messenger of God, we will set her free for your sake." Then, the Messenger of God said, "Praise be to God, I haven't seen twelve Dirhams more blessed than these. For, they have clothed two naked men and freed a woman."[25]

Despite all the hardship and harm he encountered from his people – that which has never been encountered by any prophet before.[26]

He was keen on guiding them towards the Straight Path, saving them from ignorance and misguidances, and granting them a good life in this world and the Hereafter.

---

[25] Ṣadūq, Shaykh Muḥammad b. 'Alī, *al-Amālī*, p. 308, al-Majlis 42, ḥadīth 5.

[26] In reference to the popular ḥadīth: "No prophet has been harmed like I was."

Ibn al-Maghāzlī, *Manāqīb al-Imām 'Alī b. Abī Tālib*, Vol. 3, p. 247.

'Alī b. 'Isā Hakkārī, *Kashf al-Ghumma fī Ma'rifat al-A'imma*, Vol. 2, p. 537.

And when he conquered them, he calmed them by saying, "There shall be no reproach upon you today. Go on; for, you have been set free."[27]

It has been narrated, in *al-Muwathaq*, that Imām Muḥammad al-Bāqir ؑ said, "The Messenger of God called upon the Jewish woman who poisoned the Prophet's sheep and asked her, "What made you do it?" She said, "I said to myself: If he was a prophet, then he wouldn't be harmed. And if he was a king, then I would be relieving the people from him". He

---

[27] In reference to Sūrat Yūsuf, Verse 92:

﴿قَالَ لَا تَثْرِيبَ عَلَيْكُمُ الْيَوْمَ ۖ يَغْفِرُ اللَّهُ لَكُمْ ۖ وَهُوَ أَرْحَمُ الرَّاحِمِينَ﴾

﴿*qāla lā tathrība ʿalaykumu l-yawma yaghfiru llāhu lakum wa-huwa ʾarḥamu r-rāḥimīn* [a]﴾

﴿*He said, 'There shall be no reproach on you today. God will forgive you, and He is the most merciful of the merciful*﴾

Kulaynī, Shaykh Muḥammad b. Yaʿqūb, *al-Kāfī*, Vol. 1, p. 513.

Ibn Abī Shaybah, *Muṣannaf Ibn Abī Shaybah*, Vol. 7, p. 250.

said, "Then, the Messenger of God pardoned her."[28]

Whoever takes a deep look into his attributes, speeches and actions would realize that he was the one sent to guide people from darkness towards the light.

These are only some of many attributes that are difficult to count; for, how can one count the attributes of the person whom God ﷻ glorified Himself ﷻ for the journey he took, where He ﷻ said:

﴿سُبْحَانَ الَّذِي أَسْرَىٰ بِعَبْدِهِ لَيْلًا
مِنَ الْمَسْجِدِ الْحَرَامِ إِلَى الْمَسْجِدِ الْأَقْصَى﴾

﴿subḥāna lladhī 'asrā bi-'abdihī laylan mina l-masjidi l-ḥarāmi 'ilā l-masjidi l-'aqṣā﴾

[28] Kulaynī, Shaykh Muḥammad b. Ya'qūb, *al-Kāfī*, Vol. 2, p. 108.

﴾Immaculate is He who carried His servant on a journey by night from the Sacred Mosque to the Farthest Mosque﴿,[29]

praised Himself ﷻ for the book which He ﷻ sent down to him:

﴿الْحَمْدُ لِلَّهِ الَّذِي أَنْزَلَ عَلَىٰ عَبْدِهِ الْكِتَابَ وَلَمْ يَجْعَلْ لَهُ عِوَجًا﴾

﴾l-ḥamdu li-llāhi lladhī ʾanzala ʿalā ʿabdihi l-kitāba wa-lam yajʿal lahū ʿiwajā﴿

﴾All praise belongs to God, who has sent down the Book to His servant and did not let any crookedness be in it﴿,[30]

blessed Himself ﷻ for the Criterion which He ﷻ sent down to him:

﴿تَبَارَكَ الَّذِي نَزَّلَ الْفُرْقَانَ عَلَىٰ عَبْدِهِ﴾

﴾tabāraka lladhī nazzala l-furqāna ʿalā ʿabdihī﴿

---

[29] Sūrat al-Isrāʾ, Verse 1.

[30] Sūrat al-Kahf, Verse 1.

﴾Blessed is He who sent down the Criterion to His servant﴿,[31]

and whom God ﷻ chose to converse with in the Highest Realm:

﴿فَأَوْحَىٰ إِلَىٰ عَبْدِهِ مَا أَوْحَىٰ﴾

﴾fa-ʾawḥā ʾilā ʿabdihī mā ʾawḥā﴿

﴾whereat He revealed to His servant whatever He revealed﴿[32]

The Prophet's Sermons

We will only mention the sermons he had shared with Abī Dharr:

"O' Abā Dharr, worship God as if you see Him. For, if you do not see Him, He sees you.

And let it be known to you that the first step to worshiping God is to know Him. For, He is the First to exist before anything came into

---

[31] Sūrat al-Furqān, Verse 1.

[32] Sūrat al-Najm, Verse 10.

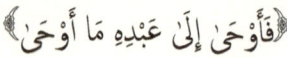

existence. Thus, nothing is before him. And He is the Singular which has no other, and the One who remains without a designated purpose. He created the heavens and earth and whatever lies within the, and amongst them. He is God – the Most-Gentle and the All-Aware. And He has power over all things.

Then, [the second step] is to believe in me and admit that God ﷻ had sent me to all mankind as a bearer of good news, a warner, one who calls people towards God with His permission and a luminous lantern.

Then, [the third step] is the love of my Ahl al-Bayt (progeny) whom God repelled all impurities from them and purified them thoroughly.

You must know, O' Abā Dharr, that God has made my Ahl al-Bayt in my nation like the Ark of Nūḥ; whoever rides in it will be saved, and whoever chooses another path will drown. They are also like the Gate of Repentance of the Children of Israel (*Banū Isrā'īl*); whoever enters through the gate will be safe.

O' Abā Dharr, safeguard that which I am advising you, and you will be happy in this world and the Hereafter.

O' Abā Dharr, there are two blessings that are taken for granted by mankind - health and spare time.

O' Abā Dharr, take advantage of five things before five things seize you: your youth before your old age, your health before your sickness, your wealth before your poverty, your spare time before your business and your life before your death.

O' Abā Dharr, beware of procrastination; for, you live today and not tomorrow. If tomorrow rises upon you, then be in that moment as you are today. And if it doesn't, then you will grievously regret the opportunity you missed today.

O' Abā Dharr, how many people started their day without completing it! And how many people eagerly await their tomorrow yet never realize it!

O' Abā Dharr, surely God's rights (upon us) are greater than His servant can possibly fulfill! And surely the favors of God are more than His servants can ever encompass. This is why they spend their nights and days in repentance.

O' Abā Dharr, do not look at the triviality of the sin; rather, look at whom you have disobeyed.

O' Abā Dharr, as long as you are in prayer you are knocking on the door of the Great King; and whoever knocks much on the door of the King, it will eventually open.

O' Abā Dharr, there isn't any believer who stands in prayer except that goodness (*Birr*) befalls him from the Throne. And an angel is appointed for him that calls out, "Oh son of Adam, if you knew what you got out of your prayer and whom you were calling, you would not turn away."

O' Abā Dharr, God says, "I do not put my servant through fear or safety in both worlds; that is, if he feels safe from Me in this world, I will make him fear Me on the Day of Resurrection. And if he fears Me in this world, I will bestow upon him safety on the Day of Resurrection."

O' Abā Dharr, Jibrā'īl came to me with the treasures of the world upon a gray mule and said, "O' Muḥammad! These are the treasures of the world (brought to you); they will not undermine your share (in the Hereafter) with your Lord." I said, "My beloved Jibrā'īl! I have no need for them. When I'm satiated, I thank my Lord; and when I'm hungry I ask Him."

O' Abā Dharr, when God wants to do his servant any good, He makes him knowledgeable in his religion, abstemious in this world and mindful of his own faults.

O' Abā Dharr, let there be an intention in everything you do, even in sleeping and eating.

O' Abā Dharr, there isn't any young man who forsakes this world and its distractions for the sake of God, and grows into old age upon the obedience of God, except that God bestows upon him the reward of seventy two righteous men.

O' Abā Dharr, God is present at the speech of every speaker; thus, let him fear God in his words and let him be aware of what he speaks.

O' Abā Dharr, the most beloved to God from amongst you are those who remember God the most. And the most privileged from amongst you, in God's eyes, are the most God-weary.

And the safest from His punishment are the most fearful of Him.

O' Abā Dharr, he who comes on the Day of Resurrection without the following three attributes has lost. I said: May my father and mother be sacrificed for you, what are those three attributes? He said: Piety which prevents him from committing any of God's prohibitions, patience through which he deals with the fool's ignorance and good morality with which he humors people.

O' Abā Dharr, if it pleases you to be the strongest of mankind then rely on God ; and if it pleases you to be the most generous of mankind then be wary of God. If it pleases you to be the richest of mankind then be more confident of what lies in God's hands than of what lies in yours.

O' Abā Dharr, had people abided by this verse, it would have sufficed them:

﴿وَمَنْ يَتَّقِ اللَّهَ يَجْعَلْ لَهُ مَخْرَجًا﴾

﴿*wa-man yattaqi llāha yaj'al lahū makhraja* ^{n}﴾

﴿وَيَرْزُقْهُ مِنْ حَيْثُ لَا يَحْتَسِبُ ۚ وَمَنْ يَتَوَكَّلْ عَلَى اللَّهِ فَهُوَ
حَسْبُهُ ۚ إِنَّ اللَّهَ بَالِغُ أَمْرِهِ ۚ قَدْ جَعَلَ اللَّهُ لِكُلِّ شَيْءٍ قَدْرًا﴾

﴿*wa-yarzuqhu min ḥaythu lā yaḥtasibu wa-man yatawakkal 'alā llāhi fa-huwa ḥasbuhū 'inna llāha bālighu 'amrihī qad ja'ala llāhu li-kulli shay'in qadra* ^{n}﴾

﴿*And whoever is wary of God, He shall make a way out for him, and provide for him from whence he does not reckon. And whoever puts his trust in God, He will suffice him. Indeed God carries through His command. Certainly God has set a measure for everything*﴾[33]

---

[33] Sūrat al-Ṭalāq, Verses 2-3.

O' Abā Dharr, blessed is he who humbles himself before God without having a shortcoming, humiliates himself without being in poverty, doesn't spend his money which he has collected in sin, is merciful with the humiliated and poor, and interacts with those of knowledge and wisdom.

Blessed is he whose core is virtuous and uncorrupt and exterior is good and decent, and who holds his evil away from people.

Blessed is he who acts upon his knowledge, spends what remains from his money and keeps hold of his excessive speech to himself."[34]

It is of no surprise for Abū Dharr, who took these pieces of advice to heart and disciplined himself with these manners, to confront falsehood with righteousness and be indifferent towards threats until he was exiled from his homeland and until the Messenger of God's ﷺ words in Abū Dharr came to life when he said,

---

[34] Majlisī, 'Allamah Muḥammad Bāqir, *Biḥār al-Anwār*, Vol. 74, p. 74,

Ṭabrisī, Shaykh Faḍl b. Ḥasan, *Makārim al-Akhlāq*, p. 459.

"He lives by himself, dies by himself, gets resurrected by himself and enters heaven by himself.[35]

Moreover, attractive offers did not get through to him. For, 'Uthmān had sent him two agents who carried two hundred Dinars, and he told them, "Go to Abū Dharr and tell him 'Uthmān sends his greetings to you and tells you, behold these two hundred Dinars; they are yours to support you in your afflictions." Thereupon, Abū Dharr said, "Did he give any of the Muslims what he has given me?" They told him:, "No." He said, "Indeed, I am but one of the Muslims and, therefore, I endure that which they endure." They said, "He says that the money is of his own and that, by God who there is no God but Him, they have not been mixed with prohibited money; and they have been sent to you as purely permissible (ḥalāl) money." He said, "I have no need for it; as I have woken up this morning as the richest of mankind." They told him, "May God grant you good health and improve your condition! We do not see in your house anything that can be enjoyed." He said,

[35] al-Kashshī, Muḥammad b. 'Umar, *Ikhtīyār Ma'rifat al-Rijāl*, Vol. 1, p. 98, Abū Dharr 48.

"Yes, there is. Underneath this saddle which you see, there is a loaf of barley that has been laying there for days..."[36]

Furthermore, 'Uthmān had sent a bag of Dirhams with one of his slaves to Abū Dharr and told him, "If he accepts this bag, then you are to be a free man." The boy, then, came with the bag to Abū Dharr and insisted upon him to accept it, however, he didn't. So, he told him, "Accept this bag; for, with your acceptance I become a free man." Abū Dharr said, "Yes, but if I accepted it, I become a slave."[37]

His Meeting with the Higher Companion

The Messenger of God ﷺ – as narrated in *al-Tahdhīb*[38] by Shaykh al-Ṭā'ifa - has departed this

---

36 al-Kashshī, Muḥammad b. 'Umar, *Ikhtīyār Ma'rifat al-Rijāl*, Vol. 1, p. 118, Abū Dharr 53.

37 al-Bahā'i, *Likashkūl*, Vol. 1, p. 208.

38 Shaykh Muḥammad b. Ḥasan Ṭūsī, *Tahdhīb al-Ahkām fī Sharh al-Muqni'ah*, Vol. 6, p. 2.

Mufīd, Shaykh Muḥammad b. Muḥammad, *Kitāb al-Mazār*, Ch. 1.

world by being poisoned on a Monday, two nights away from the end of Ṣafar, year 10 AH.

We apologize for narrating what had happened at the moment of his death; and we will limit this narration to some of what has been mentioned in *al-Ṣiḥaḥ* and *al-Masānid*. It is narrated by ʻAbdullāh b. ʻAbbās that he said, "When the Prophet's pain became severe, he said, "Bring me a piece of paper so I can write to you a letter after which you shall never go astray." ʻUmar said, "The Prophet has been overwhelmed with pain and we have the book of God which will suffice." Then, they disagreed amongst each other and misunderstandings took place. So, the Prophet said, "Leave me; for you must not argue in front of me." Thus, Ibn ʻAbbās left as he was saying: "The greatest calamity is that which stood in between the Messenger of God and his letter."[39]

It was narrated by ʻUbaydullāh b. ʻAbdullāh that Ibn ʻAbbās had said, When the Messenger of God came, and there were men in the house, he ﷺ said: "Let me write you a letter after which

[39] Bukhārī, Muḥammad b. Ismāʻīl, *Ṣaḥīḥ Bukhārī*, Vol. 1, p. 37.

you shall never go astray." Some of them said, "The Prophet ﷺ is overwhelmed with pain and you have the Noble Qur'ān with you. The book of God shall suffice us..."[40]

It was mentioned in *Ṣaḥīḥ al-Bukhārī* that Suʿayd b. Jubayr said that Ibn 'Abbās said, "Thursday, O' Thursday!" Then, he cried until his tears soaked the gravel beneath him; and he said, "On Thursday, the Prophet's pain intensified, so he said, "Bring me a piece of paper so I can write you a letter after which you shall never go astray." Thereupon, they quarreled – when it's not acceptable to argue in the presence of a prophet – until they said that the Messenger of God had lost his consciousness..." [41]

It was mentioned in *Ṣaḥīḥ al-Bukhārī* that Suʿayd b. Jubayr said that Ibn 'Abbās said, "Thursday, O' Thursday!" Then, he cried until his tears soaked the pebbles beneath him. I said, "O' Ibn 'Abbās , what happened on Thursday?"

---

40 Bukhārī, Muḥammad b. Ismāʿīl, *Ṣaḥīḥ Bukhārī*, Vol. 7, p. 9 and Vol. 8, p. 161.

41 Bukhārī, Muḥammad b. Ismāʿīl, *Ṣaḥīḥ Bukhārī*, Vol. 4, p. 31.

He said, "the Prophet's pain intensified, so he said, "Bring me a piece of paper so I can write you a letter after which you shall never go astray." Thereupon, they quarreled – when it's not acceptable to argue in the presence of a prophet; then they said, What happened? Did he lose his consciousness? Ask him to clarify things for us. So, he said, "Leave me; for, the place I am in right now is better than that towards which you are calling me".[42]

Furthermore, *Ṣaḥīḥ al-Bukhārī* mentioned - in the chapter of the Prophet's ﷺ illness and death - two narrations. The first narration is on behalf of Saʿīd b. Jubayr, where he said: Ibn ʿAbbās said, "Thursday, O' Thursday! The Prophet's ﷺ pain intensified, so he said: "Bring me a piece of paper so I can write you a letter after which you shall never go astray." Thereupon, they quarreled – when it's not acceptable to argue in the presence of a prophet; then they said, "What happened? Did he lose his consciousness? Ask him to clarify things for us." So, he ﷺ said, "Leave me; for, the place I am in right now is

[42] Bukhārī, Muḥammad b. Ismāʿīl, *Ṣaḥīḥ Bukhārī*, Vol. 4, p. 65.

better than that towards which you are calling me."[43]

Moreover, Muslim narrated it in the book of *al-Wasiyya* while referring to three references.[44]

It is mentioned, in *Musnad Aḥmad b. Ḥanbal*, that Jābir said that the Prophet ﷺ called – on his deathbed – for a sheet so he could write a letter after which they should never go astray after him. He said: "'Umar b. al-Khaṭṭāb objected to it until he rejected it utterly."[45]

---

[43] Bukhārī, Muḥammad b. Ismā'īl, *Ṣaḥīḥ Bukhārī*, Vol. 5, p. 137.

[44] *Ṣaḥīḥ Muslim*, Vol. 5, p. 75-76. This ḥadīth was mentioned in the context of abandonment in other references that were intended for the general population such as: *Musnad Aḥmad*, Vol. 1, p. 222, 355; al-Bayhaqī, *al-Sunan al-Kubrā*, Vol. 9, p. 207; 'Abd al-Razzāq, *al-Muṣannaf*, Vol. 6, p. 57 and Vol. 10, p. 361; *Musnad al-Ḥamīdī*, Vol. 1, p. 241; *Musnad Abī Ya'la*, Vol. 4, p. 298; *al-Mu'jam al-Kabīr*, Vol. 11, p. 30, 352; *Tārīkh al-Tabarī*, Vol. 2, p. 436; *al-Bidāya wal-Nihāya*, Vol. 5, p. 247; al-Nisā'ī, Aḥmad b. Shu'ayb, *Sunan al-Kubra* Vol. 3, p. 433, 435, and other references intended for the general public.

[45] *Musnad Aḥmad b. Ḥanbal*, Vol. 3, p. 346.

Ibn al-Athīr tackled the term "lost his consciousness", in *al-Nihāya fi Gharīb al-Ḥadīth w al-Athār*, where he said that in the ḥadīth on the Prophet's ﷺ illness, the phrase "They said, what happened to him? Did he lose consciousness?" means that they were asking whether his words changed under the influence of his illness, that is to say, did his speech change and lose balance due to the influence of his illness? And that was the best of what was said in that regard. It is not considered to be informative, so it has been uttered either out of obscenity or hallucination; and the speaker was 'Umar – who doesn't meet these conditions.[46]

---

[46] ash-Shaybānī, Majd ad-Dīn Ibn al-Athīr, *al-Nihāya fi Gharīb al-Ḥadīth wal-Athār*, Vol. 5, p. 245.

In regards to specialized references, see:

1. *al-Īḍāḥ*, p. 359
2. al-Mufīd, Shaykh Muḥammad b. Muḥammad, *al-Amālī*, p. 36
3. al-Mufīd, Shaykh Muḥammad b. Muḥammad, *Awā'il al-Maqālāt*, p. 406
4. al-Mufīd, Shaykh Muḥammad b. Muḥammad, *Kitāb al-Irshād*, Vol. 1, p. 184
5. *al-Mustarshid*, p. 681-682
6. al-Ṭabrisī, Shaykh Aḥmad b. 'Alī, *al-Iḥtijāj*, Vol. 1, p. 223
7. *Sa'd al-Sa'ūd*, p. 297, and other references.

There are several points that call for reflection in regards to this issue:

First: Obeying the Messenger ﷺ is an obligation imposed by God ﷻ in the Noble Qur'ān which associated it with the obedience to God ﷻ. This was mentioned in several verses, such as the following:

﴿وَأَطِيعُوا اللَّهَ وَالرَّسُولَ لَعَلَّكُمْ تُرْحَمُونَ﴾

﴿wa-'aṭī'ū llāha wa-r-rasūla
la'allakum turḥamūn [a]*﴾*

﴿And obey God and the Apostle so that you may be granted [His] mercy﴾[47]

and

﴿وَأَطِيعُوا اللَّهَ وَأَطِيعُوا الرَّسُولَ ۚ فَإِنْ تَوَلَّيْتُمْ فَإِنَّمَا
عَلَىٰ رَسُولِنَا الْبَلَاغُ الْمُبِينُ﴾

[47] Sūrat Āl 'Imrān, Verse 132.

﴾wa-ʾaṭīʿū llāha wa-ʾaṭīʿū r-rasūla fa-ʾin tawallaytum fa-ʾinnamā ʿalā rasūlinā l-balāghu l-mubīn u﴿

﴾Obey God and obey the Apostle; but if you turn away, then Our Apostle's duty is only to communicate in clear terms﴿[48]

The purpose of making this obligation absolute lies in not limiting it to any condition or circumstance.

For God ﷻ has emphasized on the obligation of obeying Him in several verses such as the following:

﴾إِنِّي لَكُمْ رَسُولٌ أَمِينٌ﴿

﴾ʾinnī lakum rasūlun ʾamīn un﴿

﴾فَاتَّقُوا اللَّهَ وَأَطِيعُونِ﴿

﴾fa-ttaqū llāha wa-ʾaṭīʿūn i﴿

---

[48] Sūrat al-Taghābun, Verse 12.

﴾*Undeed, I am a trusted apostle [sent] to you. So, be wary of God and obey me*﴿[49]

God ﷻ associated the obedience of the Prophet ﷺ with obeying Him ﷻ, whereby He ﷻ said:

﴿مَنْ يُطِعِ الرَّسُولَ فَقَدْ أَطَاعَ اللَّهَ﴾

﴾*man yuṭiʿi r-rasūla fa-qad ʾaṭāʿa llāha*﴿

﴾*Whoever obeys the Apostle certainly obeys God*﴿[50]

Therefore, he who does not obey the Messenger ﷺ has stepped out of God's ﷻ obedience.

Second: Saying that "pain has overwhelmed him and we have the book of God" after he ﷺ has given the order "give me a piece of paper" is considered to be a form of disobeying the Messenger ﷺ.

---

[49] Sūrat al-Shuʿarāʾ, Verses 143-144.

[50] Sūrat al-Nisāʾ, Verse 80.

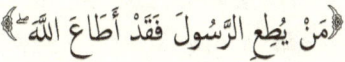

And God ﷻ said:

﴿إِذَا تَنَاجَيْتُمْ فَلَا تَتَنَاجَوْا بِالْإِثْمِ
وَالْعُدْوَانِ وَمَعْصِيَتِ الرَّسُولِ﴾

﴿ʾidhā tanājaytum fa-lā tatanājaw bi-l-ʾithmi wa-l-ʿudwāni wa-maʿṣiyati r-rasūli﴾

﴿When you talk secretly, do not hold secret talks [imbued] with sin and aggression and disobedience to the Apostle﴾[51]

And it is considered a form of disobeying God ﷻ Himself:

﴿وَمَا آتَاكُمُ الرَّسُولُ فَخُذُوهُ وَمَا نَهَاكُمْ عَنْهُ فَانْتَهُوا﴾

﴿wa-mā ʾātākumu r-rasūlu fa-khudhūhu wa-mā nahākum ʿanhu fa-ntahū﴾

﴿Take whatever the Apostle gives you, and relinquish whatever he forbids you﴾[52]

---

[51] Sūrat al-Mujādilah, Verse 9.

[52] Sūrat al-Ḥashr, Verse 7.

Moreover, God ﷻ said:

﴿وَمَنْ يَعْصِ اللَّهَ وَرَسُولَهُ فَقَدْ ضَلَّ ضَلَالًا مُبِينًا﴾

﴾wa-man ya'ṣi llāha wa-rasūlahū fa-qad ḍalla ḍalālan mubīna n﴿

﴾And whoever disobeys God and His Apostle has certainly strayed into manifest error﴿[53]

and

﴿وَمَنْ يَعْصِ اللَّهَ وَرَسُولَهُ فَإِنَّ لَهُ نَارَ جَهَنَّمَ خَالِدِينَ فِيهَا أَبَدًا﴾

﴾wa-man ya'ṣi llāha wa-rasūlahū fa-'inna lahū nāra jahannama khālidīna fīhā 'abada n﴿

﴾And whoever disobeys God and His apostle, indeed there will be for him the fire of hell, to remain in it forever﴿[54]

[53] Sūrat al-Aḥzāb, Verse 36.

[54] Sūrat al-Jinn, Verse 23.

Third: Whatever the Messenger ﷺ chooses is chosen by God, as well, according to reason and the Noble Qur'ān.

For, God ﷻ said:

﴿وَمَا كَانَ لِمُؤْمِنٍ وَلَا مُؤْمِنَةٍ إِذَا قَضَى اللَّهُ وَرَسُولُهُ أَمْرًا أَنْ يَكُونَ لَهُمُ الْخِيَرَةُ مِنْ أَمْرِهِمْ﴾

﴿*wa-mā kāna li-mu'minin wa-lā mu'minatin 'idhā qaḍā llāhu wa-rasūluhū 'amran 'an yakūna lahumu l-khiyaratu min 'amrihim*﴾

﴿*A faithful man or woman may not, when God and His Apostle have decided on a matter, have any option in their matter*﴾[55]

The term "may not" is a warning that intends to highlight the fact that this ruling may not be violated regardless of the circumstances. This verse has also associated this ruling with faith, despite it being addressed to believers and others on the basis of reason, to declare that choosing other than what God ﷻ and His Messenger ﷺ have chosen discloses absence of faith.

---

[55] Sūrat al-Aḥzāb, Verse 36.

Fourth: This saying harms the Prophet ﷺ and violated God's ﷻ words when He ﷻ said:

﴿مَا ضَلَّ صَاحِبُكُمْ وَمَا غَوَىٰ﴾

﴿*mā ḍalla ṣāḥibukum wa-mā ghawā*﴾

﴿وَمَا يَنْطِقُ عَنِ الْهَوَىٰ﴾

﴿*wa-mā yanṭiqu ʿani l-hawā*﴾

﴿*Your companion has neither gone astray, nor gone amiss. Nor does he speak out of [his own] desire*﴾[56]

The intensity of harm inflicted upon the Prophet ﷺ and its impact on him were clearly manifested, whereby he asked them to leave by saying: "Leave me", even though it was well-known that whenever someone shook his hand, the Prophet ﷺ would not let go of the person's hand until that person removes his hand first,[57] and if someone sits with him, he wouldn't get

[56] Sūrat al-Najm, Verses 2-3.

[57] Kulaynī, Shaykh Muḥammad b. Yaʿqūb, *al-Kāfī*, Vol. 2, p. 671.

up before that person leaves the gathering first.[58]

Therefore, his words "Leave me" shows the level of pain he felt at that moment, whereby he could no longer endure their presence. God ﷻ said:

﴿وَالَّذِينَ يُؤْذُونَ رَسُولَ اللَّهِ لَهُمْ عَذَابٌ أَلِيمٌ﴾

﴿wa-lladhīna yu'dhūna rasūla llāhi lahum ʿadhābun 'alīm un﴾

﴿As for those who torment the Apostle of God, there is a painful punishment for them﴾[59]

And He ﷻ said:

﴿إِنَّ الَّذِينَ يُؤْذُونَ اللَّهَ وَرَسُولَهُ لَعَنَهُمُ اللَّهُ فِي الدُّنْيَا وَالْآخِرَةِ﴾

﴿'inna lladhīna yu'dhūna llāha wa-rasūlahū laʿanahumu llāhu fī d-dunyā wa-l-'ākhirati﴾

---

[58] Ṭabrisī, Shaykh Faḍl b. Ḥasan, *Makārim al-Akhlāq*, p. 17.

[59] Sūrat al-Tawbah, Verse 61.

﴾*Indeed those who torment God and His Apostle are cursed by God in the world and the Hereafter*﴿[60]

Fifth: This saying led to the rise of high-pitched voices in the presence of the Prophet ﷺ, meanwhile God ﷻ said:

﴿يَا أَيُّهَا الَّذِينَ آمَنُوا لَا تَرْفَعُوا أَصْوَاتَكُمْ فَوْقَ صَوْتِ النَّبِيِّ﴾

﴾*yā-ʾayyuhā lladhīna ʾāmanū lā tarfaʿū ʾaṣwātakum fawqa ṣawti n-nabiyyi*﴿

﴾*O you who have faith! Do not raise your voices above the voice of the Prophet*﴿[61]

and

﴿إِنَّ الَّذِينَ يَغُضُّونَ أَصْوَاتَهُمْ عِندَ رَسُولِ اللَّهِ أُولَٰئِكَ الَّذِينَ امْتَحَنَ اللَّهُ قُلُوبَهُمْ لِلتَّقْوَىٰ﴾

﴾*ʾinna lladhīna yaghuḍḍūna ʾaṣwātahum ʿinda rasūli llāhi ʾulāʾika lladhīna mtaḥana llāhu qulūbahum li-t-taqwā*﴿

---

60 Sūrat al-Aḥzāb, Verse 57.

61 Sūrat al-Ḥujurāt, Verse 2.

﴾Indeed those who lower their voices in the presence of the Apostle of God — they are the ones whose hearts God has tested for God-wariness﴿[62]

Moreover, this saying became a reason for which they argued in the presence of the Prophet ﷺ, whereas God ﷻ had said:

﴿وَأَطِيعُوا اللَّهَ وَرَسُولَهُ وَلَا تَنَازَعُوا فَتَفْشَلُوا﴾

﴾wa-ʾaṭīʿū llāha wa-rasūlahū wa-lā tanāzaʿū fa-tafshalū﴿

﴾And obey God and His Apostle, and do not dispute, or you will lose heart﴿[63]

and He ﷻ said:

﴿يَا أَيُّهَا الَّذِينَ آمَنُوا أَطِيعُوا اللَّهَ وَأَطِيعُوا الرَّسُولَ﴾

﴾yā-ʾayyuhā lladhīna ʾāmanū ʾaṭīʿū llāha wa-ʾaṭīʿū r-rasūla﴿

---

[62] Sūrat al-Ḥujurāt, Verse 3.

[63] Sūrat al-Anfāl, Verse 46.

﴾*O you who have faith!*
Obey God and obey the Apostle﴿[64]

Thus, things unfolded such that the person whom God ﷻ entrusted with the leadership of all matters was disobeyed in his command!

Sixth: The ultimate purpose behind sending messengers and Holy Books is to guide the human being and safeguard him from going astray.

﴿هُوَ الَّذِي أَرْسَلَ رَسُولَهُ بِالْهُدَىٰ وَدِينِ الْحَقِّ﴾

﴾*huwa lladhī ʾarsala rasūlahū bi-l-hudā*
wa-dīni l-ḥaqqi﴿

﴾*It is He who has sent His Apostle with the guidance and the religion of truth*﴿[65]

---

64 Sūrat al-Nisāʾ, Verse 59.

65 Sūrat al-Tawbah, Verse 33.

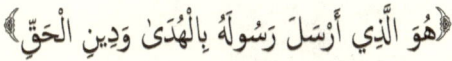

And the supplication that is mentioned in the beginning of the Noble Qur'ān and which is whispered in every prayer by every Muslim is:

﴿اهْدِنَا الصِّرَاطَ الْمُسْتَقِيمَ﴾

﴿*ⁱ hdinā ṣ-ṣirāṭa l-mustaqīm ᵃ*﴾

﴿صِرَاطَ الَّذِينَ أَنْعَمْتَ عَلَيْهِمْ غَيْرِ الْمَغْضُوبِ عَلَيْهِمْ وَلَا الضَّالِّينَ﴾

﴿*ṣirāṭa lladhīna 'an'amta 'alayhim ghayri l-maghḍūbi 'alayhim wa-lā ḍ-ḍāllīn ᵃ*﴾

﴾Guide us on the straight path, the path of those whom You have blessed—such as* have not incurred Your wrath,* nor are astray*﴿*[66]

Moreover, the Prophet ﷺ who foresaw the trials that will befall his nation after him felt empathetic towards his nation and wanted to protect them from misguidance after having been guided, through a letter which guarantees

---

[66] Sūrat al-Fātiḥa, Verses 6-7.

* For further Qur'ānic references to 'those whom God has blessed,' see 4:69 and 19:58; see also 5:23, 110; 12:6; 27:19; 28:17; 43:59; 48:2.

* This is in accordance with the *qirā'ah* of 'Āṣim, *ghayril-maghḍūbi*, which appears in the Arabic text above. However, in accordance with an alternative, and perhaps preferable, reading *ghayral-maghḍūbi* (attributed to Imam 'Alī b. Abī Ṭālib ﵇ as well as to Ibn Mas'ūd and Ubayy b. Ka'b among the Companions, and to Ibn Kathīr al-Makkī, among the seven authorities of *qirā'ah*), the translation will be: 'not of those who have incurred Your wrath, nor those who are astray.' (see *Mu'jam al-Qirā'āt al-Qur'āniyyah*).

* For further references to 'those who incur God's wrath,' see 4:93; 5:60; 7:71, 152; 8:16; 16:106; 20:81; 42:16; 48:6; 58:14; 60:13.

* For further references to 'those who are astray,' see 2:108, 175; 3:90; 4:116, 136, 167; 5:12, 60, 77; 6:74, 77, 125, 140; 7:30, 179; 14:3, 18, 27; 15:56; 17:72, 97; 19:38; 22:4, 12; 23:106; 25:44; 28:50; 31:11; 33:36, 67; 34:8; 36:47; 38:26; 39:22; 40:34; 41:52; 42:18; 45:23; 46:5, 32; 60:1.

their safety from misguidance, whereby he said: "So I could write you a letter after which you shall not go astray." He based the 'protection from misguidance' on the letter, which indicates that by missing out on that letter, the nation was deprived from the greatest blessings which is the blessing of guidance, and that it was afflicted by the worst of afflictions which is misguidance!

Seventh: Saying "the Noble Qur'ān suffices us" goes against the Noble Qur'ān, the Sunnah, scholastic unanimity and reason. It violates the Noble Qur'ān; for, by saying this, the obligation of obeying the Prophet ﷺ and the prohibition of disobeying him were rendered pointless. Meanwhile these rulings were mentioned in the Noble Qur'ān:

﴿وَمَا آتَاكُمُ الرَّسُولُ فَخُذُوهُ وَمَا نَهَاكُمْ عَنْهُ فَانْتَهُوا﴾

﴿wa-mā 'ātākumu r-rasūlu fa-khudhūhu wa-mā nahākum 'anhu fa-ntahū﴾

﴾*Take whatever the Apostle gives you, and relinquish whatever he forbids you*﴿[67]

This saying also violated the absolute scholastic unanimity on the obligation of obeying the Sunnah, which was mentioned in the chapters of knowledge and others. For, had the Noble Qur'ān been sufficient, there wouldn't have been any need for all these six Siḥāḥ which – in that case – would have been a violation of the unanimous scholastic opinion on referring back to the Sunnah.

It is also considered a clear violation of reason which rules that one cannot benefit from the detailed provisions in regards to acts of worship, transactions and policies if he were to limit himself to the slogan "We have the book of God which suffices us".

The declaration made by al-Dhahabī emphasizes on what was mentioned above. For, he said that "the book of God suffices us" is a saying repeated by al-Khawārij,[68] and it

---

[67] Sūrat al-Ḥashr, Verse 7.

[68] al-Dhahabī, *Tadhkirat al-Hifāẓ*, Vol..1, p. 3.

overlooked what was mentioned in several chapters of *Ṣaḥīḥ al-Bukhārī* and other *Siḥāḥ* and *Masānid*.

Eighth: The Prophet ﷺ was sent to all of mankind; and his nation remains until the Day of Resurrection. He wanted to write a letter so that the nation does not go astray after him. Pursuant to which right, then, did he prevent him from fulfilling this action and deprive the nation's right (of guidance) by saying "We have the book of God and it suffices us"?!

Nineth: Muslim narrated - on behalf of 'Abdul Raḥmān b. Abza - that a man came to 'Umar and said: "I entered the state of Janābah, then I did not find water. So, 'Umar said, "Do not pray." Then, 'Ammār said, "Don't you recall, O' 'Amīr al-Mu'minīn, when you and I went on a military expedition where we entered a state of *Janābah* but could not find water, and you did not pray whereas I dipped myself in soil and prayed, then the Prophet ﷺ said, "It would have been sufficient to tap your hands on the ground then blow on the, and wipe your face and hands with them?" 'Umar, then, said, "Fear God, O'

ʿAmmār." He said, "If you want, I will not speak of this incident."[69]

It is not a concealed matter that prayer is the pillar of religion, to which the key is purification.

God ﷻ said:

﴿يَا أَيُّهَا الَّذِينَ آمَنُوا إِذَا قُمْتُمْ إِلَى الصَّلَاةِ فَاغْسِلُوا وُجُوهَكُمْ وَأَيْدِيَكُمْ إِلَى الْمَرَافِقِ وَامْسَحُوا بِرُءُوسِكُمْ وَأَرْجُلَكُمْ إِلَى الْكَعْبَيْنِ ۚ وَإِنْ كُنْتُمْ جُنُبًا فَاطَّهَّرُوا ۚ وَإِنْ كُنْتُمْ مَرْضَىٰ أَوْ عَلَىٰ

[69] Muslim b. al-Ḥajjāj, *Ṣaḥīḥ Muslim*, Vol. 1, p. 193; *Musnad Aḥmad b. Ḥanbal*, Vol. 4, p. 265; Bukhārī, Muḥammad b. Ismāʿīl, *Ṣaḥīḥ Bukhārī*, Vol. 1, p. 87, chapter of *al-Tayammum Hal Yunfakh Fīhima;* Muḥammad b. Mājah al-Qazwīnī, *Sunan Ibn Mājah*, Vol. 1, p. 188; al-Sijistānī, Abū Dāwūd, *Sunan Abī Dāwūd*, Vol. 1, p. 81; al-Nisāʾī, Aḥmad b. Shuʿayb, *Sunan al-Nisāʾī* Vol. 1, p. 166 and 170; al-Bayhaqī, *Sunan al-Kubra lil Bayhaqī*, Vol. 1, p. 209; *ʿAwn al-Maʿbūd*, Vol. 1, p. 355; al-Ṭayālisī, Abū Dāwūd Sulaymān b. Dāwūd, *Musnad Abī Dawūd al-Ṭayālīsī*, p. 89; al-Nisāʾī, Aḥmad b. Shuʿayb, *Sunan al-Kubra*, Vol. 1, p. 134-135, *Musnad Abī Yaʿla*, Vol. 3, p. 183; *Ṣaḥīḥ Ibn Khuzaymah*, Vol. 1, p. 135; *Ṣaḥīḥ Ibn Ḥabban*, Vol. 4, p. 131-133; al-Dhahabī, *Tadhkirat al-Hifāẓ*, Vol. 3, p. 951; and other general references for the public.

سَفَرٍ أَوْ جَاءَ أَحَدٌ مِنْكُمْ مِنَ الْغَائِطِ أَوْ لَامَسْتُمُ النِّسَاءَ فَلَمْ
تَجِدُوا مَاءً فَتَيَمَّمُوا صَعِيدًا طَيِّبًا فَامْسَحُوا بِوُجُوهِكُمْ وَأَيْدِيكُمْ
مِنْهُ ۚ مَا يُرِيدُ اللَّهُ لِيَجْعَلَ عَلَيْكُمْ مِنْ حَرَجٍ وَلَٰكِنْ يُرِيدُ
لِيُطَهِّرَكُمْ وَلِيُتِمَّ نِعْمَتَهُ عَلَيْكُمْ لَعَلَّكُمْ تَشْكُرُونَ﴾

﴿yā-ʾayyuhā lladhīna ʾāmanū ʾidhā qumtum ʾilā ṣ-ṣalāti fa-ghsilū wujūhakum wa-ʾaydiyakum ʾilā l-marāfiqi wa-msaḥū bi-ruʾūsikum wa-ʾarjulakum ʾilā l-kaʿbayni wa-ʾin kuntum junuban fa-ṭṭahharū wa-ʾin kuntum marḍā ʾaw ʿalā safarin ʾaw jāʾa ʾaḥadun minkum mina l-ghāʾiṭi ʾaw lāmastumu n-nisāʾa fa-lam tajidū māʾan fa-tayammamū ṣaʿīdan ṭayyiban fa-msaḥū bi-wujūhikum wa-ʾaydīkum minhu mā yurīdu llāhu li-yajʿala ʿalaykum min ḥarajin wa-lākin yurīdu li-yuṭahhirakum wa-li-yutimma niʿmatahū ʿalaykum laʿallakum tashkurūn [a]﴾

﴿O you who have faith! When you stand up for prayer, wash your faces and your hands up to the elbows, and wipe a part of your heads and your feet, up to the ankles. If you are junub, purify yourselves. But if you are sick, or on a journey, or any of you has come from the toilet, or you have touched women, and you cannot find water, then make tayammum

with clean ground and wipe a part of your faces and your hands with it. God does not desire to put you to hardship, but He desires to purify you, and to complete His blessing upon you so that you may give thanks﴾[70]

And it is but the Prophet ﷺ who made these provisions clear for them.

Al-'Aʿmash spoke on behalf of Abī Zabyān who said that Ibn ʿAbbās said, "ʿUmar brought an afflicted woman who committed fornication and ordered to stone her, when ʿAlī b. Abī Ṭālib ﵇ passed by her and saw a group of boys escorting her. So, he asked: "What's this?" They told him that ʿUmar had ordered to have her stoned. So, he escorted her back to ʿUmar, then he ﵇ said, "Did you not know that judgment is suspended from an insane person until he becomes sane, from an afflicted person until he becomes aware, from a sleeping person until he

[70] Sūrat al-Mā'idah, Verse 6.

wakes up and from a boy until he reaches puberty?"[71]

It was narrated on behalf of 'Abdullāh b. al-Ḥasan, that he said, "'Alī came to 'Umar, and he saw a pregnant woman on her way to being stoned. He said, "What's her issue?" She said, "They are taking me to stone me". He said: "O' 'Amīr al-Mu'minīn, for what reason is she being stoned? If you have power over her, then you surely do not have any power over what's in her womb." Then, 'Umar said three times, "Everyone is more knowledgeable than me."[72]

---

[71] al-Ḥakim al-Nīshāpūrī, *al-Mustadrak 'ala al-Ṣaḥīḥayn*, Vol. 4, p. 389 and Vol. 1, p. 258, Vol. 2, p. 59; al-Sijistānī, Abū Dāwūd, *Sunan Abī Dāwūd*, Vol. 2, p. 339 with multiple references; al-Bayhaqī, *Sunan al-Kubra lil Bayhaqī*, Vol. 4, p. 269 and Vol. 8, p. 264; 'Abd al-Razzāq, *al-Muṣannaf*, Vol. 7, p. 80; *Musnad Ibn al-Ja'd*, p. 120; al-Nisā'ī, Aḥmad b. Shu'ayb, *Sunan al-Kubra*, Vol. 4, p. 323; *Musnad Abī Ya'la*, Vol. 1, p. 440; *Ṣaḥīḥ Ibn Khuzaymah*, Vol. 2, p. 102 and Vol. 4, p. 248; *Ṣaḥīḥ Ibn Ḥabban*, Vol. 1, p. 356; Bukhārī, Muḥammad b. Ismā'īl, *Ṣaḥīḥ Bukhārī*, Vol. 8, p. 21, Chapter of *Raj al-Muḥsin*; and other general references intended for the public.

[72] *Thakha'ir al-'Uqba*, p. 81; *al-Riyāḍ al-Nāḍira*, Vol. 3, p. 143; *Kifāyat al-Ṭālib*, p. 227, ch. 59.

Moreover, al-Bayhaqī narrated in his *Sunan* on behalf of al-Shaʿbī that he said: ʿUmar b. al-Khaṭṭāb delivered a speech to the people, so he praised God ﷻ and said, "Do not demand high dowries for your women. If I hear of anyone who demands or receives a dowry greater than that stated by the Messenger of God I will collect the excess amount and add it to the Treasury." Then, he came down from the platform. A Qurayshi woman came to him and said, "O' ʾAmīr al-Muʾminīn, who is more entitled of obedience, your words or the book of God?" He said, "The book of God , why?" She said, "You have just forbidden people from demanding expensive dowries.

Meanwhile God says in His Noble Qurʾān:

﴿وَآتَيْتُمْ إِحْدَاهُنَّ قِنطَارًا فَلَا تَأْخُذُوا مِنْهُ شَيْئًا﴾

﴿wa-ʾātaytum ʾiḥdāhunna qinṭāran fa-lā taʾkhudhū minhu shayʾan﴾

﴿and you have given one of them a quintal [of gold], do not take anything away from it﴾"[73]

[73] Sūrat al-Nisāʾ, Verse 20.

Then, ‘Umar said – two or three times, “Everyone is more knowledgeable than ‘Umar.”

Furthermore, it has been narrated in *al-Sunan al-Kubrā* that ‘Umar came to a woman who gave birth in her sixth month of pregnancy, so he intended on stoning her. Imām ‘Alī ﵇ was informed of this incident, so he said, “She is not to be stoned.” ‘Umar was told of Imām ‘Alī’s ﵇ response, so he sent him someone to ask him about his response, upon which the Imām ﵇ answered with the following verse:

﴿وَالْوَالِدَاتُ يُرْضِعْنَ أَوْلَادَهُنَّ حَوْلَيْنِ كَامِلَيْنِ ۖ لِمَنْ أَرَادَ أَنْ يُتِمَّ الرَّضَاعَةَ﴾

﴾*wa-l-wālidātu yurḍiʿna ʾawlādahunna ḥawlayni kāmilayni li-man ʾarāda ʾan yutimma r-raḍāʿata*﴿

﴾*Mothers shall suckle their children for two full years, —that for such as desire to complete the suckling*﴿[74]

and He ﵇ said,

[74] Sūrat al-Baqarah, Verse 233.

﴿وَحَمْلُهُ وَفِصَالُهُ ثَلَاثُونَ شَهْرًا﴾

﴾*wa-ḥamluhū wa-fiṣāluhū thalāthūna shahran*﴿

﴾*and his gestation and weaning take thirty months*﴿[75]

Therefore, these thirty months include twenty four months of gestation and six months of pregnancy which means that she is not subjected to any punishment or stoning, so – he said – he let her go.[76]

There is no doubt that a scholar is usually highly cautious with matters of bloodshed. There are also other references, however, we will stick to the above-mentioned references.

---

75 Sūrat al-Aḥqāf, Verse 15.

76 al-Bayhaqī, *Sunan al-Kubra lil Bayhaqī*, Vol. 7, p. 442; ʻAbd al-Razzāq, *al-Muṣannaf*, Vol. 7, p. 350; al-Ḥanafī, Muḥammad b. Yūsuf al-Zarandī, *Naẓm Durar al-Simṭayn*, p. 131; al-Hindī, ʻAlī al-Muttaqī, *Kanz al-ʻUmmāl fī Sunan al-Aqwāl wal-Afʻāl*, Vol. 5, p. 457, al-Suyūṭī, Jalāl al-Dīn, *al-Durr al-Manthūr* Vol. 1, p. 288 and Vol. 6, p. 40; Ibn Sabbāh, *Tārīkh al-Madīnah*, Vol. 3, p. 979; and other general references.

Is it reasonable that someone – with so little knowledge of the Noble Qur'ān – objects to the one who received God's ﷻ book and revelation by saying "the Noble Qur'ān suffices us"?

Tenth: Whoever reflects upon his ﷺ saying, "I will leave amongst you two weighty things. The book of God and my progeny. These two shall not be parted until they return to the pool [of abundance in paradise]. As long as you cling to them, you will not go astray", and his ﷺ saying, "So I could write you a letter after which you shall not go astray", will realize that this letter is complementary to that ḥadīth, so that the nation remains protected from misguidance – as he said "you shall not go astray". God bless Ibn 'Abbās who said, "The greatest calamity lies in whoever stands between the Messenger of God and his letter."

Rays from the Life of the Messenger of God ﷺ

Let us enlighten ourselves with the luminous rays of his blessed life, which is –in itself – a proof for his message and Prophethood.

When the Prophet ﷺ started calling people towards Islam, the Qurayshi tribes were afraid that people would obey him, so they exerted all sorts of pressure such as threats and promises. Then, they came together to his uncle, Abū Ṭālib, and told him, "O' Abā Ṭālib, your nephew has ridiculed our dreams, insulted our gods, corrupted our youth and caused division in our unions. If his movement is influenced by poverty, we shall collect money for him and he will become the wealthiest man in Quraysh. We will also marry him off to any Qurayshi woman of his choice." They even promised him ownership of property and positions of power.

His response ﷺ was: "If they placed the sun in my right hand and the moon in my left, I wouldn't want them."[77]

When they realized that such promises won't have an influence on him ﷺ and that he is moving forward with his mission, inattentive to their promises, they went for threats and inflicting harm.

Below are some examples:

When the Prophet ﷺ used to stand in al-Masjid al-Ḥarām for prayer, they would send him four of Banī 'Abd al-Dār who were the military

---

[77] al-Qummī, 'Alī b. Ibrāhīm, *Tafsīr al-Qummī*, Vol. 1, p. 228.

﴿وَعَجِبُوا أَنْ جَاءَهُمْ مُنْذِرٌ مِنْهُمْ ۖ وَقَالَ الْكَافِرُونَ هَٰذَا سَاحِرٌ كَذَّابٌ﴾

﴾wa-'ajibū 'an jā'ahum mundhirun minhum wa-qāla l-kāfirūna hādhā sāḥirun kadhdhāb un﴿

﴾They consider it odd that there should come to them a warner from among themselves, and the faithless say, 'This is a magician, a mendacious liar.'﴿

Sūrat Ṣād, Verse 4.

leaders of Quraysh. Two would stand on his right and whistle, and two would stand on his left and clap their hands to annoy him and distract him from prayer![78]

Once, on his way to the mosque, they threw dirt at his head; and when he was in prostration they threw a sheep's womb on his back. Then, his daughter came to him, removed it and wiped his

---

[78] Ṭabrisī, Shaykh Faḍl b. Ḥasan, *Majmaʿ al-Bayān fī Tafsīr al-Qur'ān,* Vol. 4, p. 463.

﴿وَمَا كَانَ صَلَاتُهُمْ عِندَ الْبَيْتِ إِلَّا مُكَاءً وَتَصْدِيَةً﴾

﴿wa-mā kāna ṣalātuhum ʿinda l-bayti 'illā mukā'an wa-taṣdiyatan﴾

﴿Their prayer at the House is nothing but whistling and clapping﴾

Sūrat al-'Anfāl, Verse 35.

back clean; for, he did not raise his head from prostration.[79]

After the death of his uncle and supporter, Abū Ṭālib, the afflictions that had befallen him intensified and Quraysh's cruelty against him increased. For, in such dangerous circumstances, the Prophet ﷺ went to the tribe of Thaqīf in al-Ṭā'if and asked them to protect him until he delivers the message of his Lord. However, they refused to do that, ridiculed him and attacked him through their fools and boys. They blocked his way by making two lines such that whenever the Messenger of God ﷺ passed, they would wound his legs with stones until they would bleed. He made it through these lines with bloody feet; then, he headed towards

---

[79] al-'Ayyāshī, Muḥammad b. Mas'ūd, *Tafsīr al-'Ayyāshī*, Vol. 2, p. 43, in the interpretation of His verse:

﴿وَاللَّهُ خَيْرُ الْمَاكِرِينَ﴾

﴾*wa-llāhu khayru l-mākirīn* [a]﴿

﴾*And God is the best of devisers*﴿

Sūrat Āl 'Imrān, Verse 54.

their walls and sat in the shade of one of the palm trees while enduring the pain of his bleeding feet. Next to the wall stood ʿUtba b. Rabīʿa and Shība b. Rabīʿa, when he saw them he felt annoyed as he knew their hatred and animosity towards God ﷻ and his Messenger ﷺ. When they saw him, they sent him a boy called ʿOdās carrying some grapes. ʿOdās was a Christian boy from the city of Naynawā. Then he came to the Messenger of God, and he ﷺ asked him, "From which city are you?" He said, "From Naynawā." He said, "From the city of the virtuous man, Yūnus b. Mattā?" ʿOdās said, "What do you know about Yūnus b. Mattā?" He ﷺ said, "I am the Messenger of God. And God told me about Yūnus b. Mattā." Then, when he ﷺ told him about the revelation that was sent to him by God ﷻ in regards to Yūnus ﷺ, ʿOdās bowed in prostration to God ﷻ and in glorification of the Messenger of God ﷺ,

whereby he started to kiss his feet as they were dripping in blood.[80]

Moreover, they harmed his companions using all means of torture. For, they used to lay Bilāl under the scorching sun and place a heavy rock on his chest then ask him to speak words of

---

[80] Ibn al-Maghāzlī, *Manāqīb al-Imām ʿAlī b. Abī Tālib*, Vol. 1, p. 68.

Ṭabrisī, Shaykh Faḍl b. Ḥasan, *Majmaʿ al-Bayān fī Tafsīr al-Qur'ān*, Vol. 9, p. 154.

In reference to Sūrat al-Aḥqāf, Verse 30:

﴿قَالُوا يَا قَوْمَنَا إِنَّا سَمِعْنَا كِتَابًا أُنْزِلَ مِنْ بَعْدِ مُوسَىٰ مُصَدِّقًا لِمَا بَيْنَ يَدَيْهِ يَهْدِي إِلَى الْحَقِّ وَإِلَىٰ طَرِيقٍ مُسْتَقِيمٍ﴾

﴾*qālū yā-qawmanā 'innā samiʿnā kitāban 'unzila min baʿdi mūsā muṣaddiqan li-mā bayna yadayhi yahdī 'ilā l-ḥaqqi wa-'ilā ṭarīqin mustaqīm* in﴿

﴾*They said, 'O our people! Indeed we have heard a Book which has been sent down after Moses, confirming what was before it. It guides to the truth and to a straight path*﴿

disbelief; however, he would repeat: [He is only] One, only One![81]

They also tortured Sumayyā, 'Ammār's elderly mother, so she would abandon her religion and disbelieve; nonetheless, she didn't so they killed her![82]

Yet, despite all this harm, when the companions asked the Prophet ﷺ – in certain situations – to curse his nation, he said, "Indeed, I was sent as God's mercy to mankind."[83] He would rather pray for them "O' God, guide my nation; for, they lack the needed knowledge."[84]

For, instead of punishment, he wished that God ﷻ would bestow upon them a mercy like no

---

[81] Aḥmad al-Isfahānī, *Ḥilyat al-Awliya' wa-Ṭabaqāt al-Aṣfiya'*, Vol. 1, p. 148.

Muḥammad al-Ṭabarī, *Tārīkh al-Ṭabarī*, Vol. 2, p. 153.

[82] *I'lām al-Warāh*, Vol. 1, p. 132, ch. five on the harm encountered by the Messenger of God ﷺ with the disbelievers.

[83] Majlisī, 'Allamah Muḥammad Bāqir, *Biḥār al-Anwār*, Vol. 8, p. 243.

[84] Sa'īd al-Kāshānī, *al-Kharā'ij wa l-Jarā'iḥ*, Vol. 1, p. 164.

other – that is, the mercy of guidance. Moreover, he associated the nation to himself by saying 'my nation', in pursuit of safeguarding them from God's ﷻ wrath and so that he can intercede for them in front of God ﷻ and ask him for forgiveness – on their behalf – rather than complain about them.

His ﷺ lifestyle was filled with asceticism and austerity. His food was composed of barley bread; and he would not eat from it until he reached fullness.[85]

The Great Righteous Lady – Sayyidah Fāṭimah al-Zahrā' عليها السلام – came to him once in the conquest of al-Khandaq with a piece of bread. So, she handed it over to the Prophet ﷺ, and he ﷺ said, "What is this piece?" She عليها السلام said, "A piece of bread which I have made for al-Ḥasan and al-Ḥusayn. I brought you a piece of that bread." So he ﷺ said, "O' Fāṭimah, this is but the first

---

[85] Ṣadūq, Shaykh Muḥammad b. 'Alī, *al-Amālī*, p. 398.

Ṭabrisī, Shaykh Faḍl b. Ḥasan, *Makārim al-Akhlāq*, p. 28.

food that enters your father's mouth since three days!"[86]

His austerity was not due to his lack of financial means; for, he used to receive in those days the money which he would divide, grant and give as alms. He would even grant a single person one hundred camels![87]

He left this world without leaving a single Dinar, Dirham, boy, bondmaid, sheep or camel. His shield was pledged to a Jewish man in exchange for twenty portions of barley which he had bought to feed his family.[88]

One must reflect upon two points:

First: There is no doubt that the Jewish man didn't ask the Prophet ﷺ for a document, due to his position and trustworthiness. However, the Prophet ﷺ intended to abide by the law of

---

[86] Ṣadūq, Shaykh Muḥammad b. ʿAlī, *ʿUyūn Akhbār al-Riḍā*, Vol. 2, p. 40, ch. 31, ḥadīth 123.

[87] Ṣadūq, Shaykh Muḥammad b. ʿAlī, *Man Lā Yaḥḍuruh al-Faqīh*, Vol. 2, p. 153.

[88] al-Ḥimyarī, ʿAbd Allāh b. Jaʿfar, *Qurb al-Isnād*, p. 91.

pledges in the absence of a written debt, so that the money may act as a document for the creditor even if the creditor was Jewish and the debtor was the greatest Islamic figure.

Second: The Prophet ﷺ had access to the most delicious food, however, it was sufficient for him to eat barley bread all his life, so that his food would not be better than the weakest of his people.

An Example of His Altruism

The position of Sayyidah Fāṭimah al-Zahrā' ﷺ is well-known amongst the elite and public. For, the books of both parties are filled with her virtues – given that she had prayed in her niche until her feet were swollen,[89] following in the footsteps of his father.

And in spite of her indulgence in worshiping God ﷻ, she would manage the house of God's Friend ﷺ and raise the children of His Messenger ﷺ, so much so that the Prophet ﷺ came to her house, one day, and saw her grinding the mill and nursing her child, which brought tears to his eyes.[90]

Imām 'Alī ﷺ once saw her filling up the water vessel in a way that affected her chest, grinding the mill until her hands were swollen and cleaning the house until her clothes were filled with dust. So, he told her, "If you ask your

---

[89] Ibn al-Maghāzlī, *Manāqib al-Imām 'Alī b. Abī Tālib*, Vol. 3, p. 341.

[90] Ibn al-Maghāzlī, *Manāqib al-Imām 'Alī b. Abī Tālib*, Vol. 3, p. 342.

Ṭabrisī, Shaykh Faḍl b. Ḥasan, *Makārim al-Akhlāq*, p. 117.

father for a servant, he would avert you from this agony."

So, she went to her father, but she felt timid and left. The Prophet ﷺ knew that she came to ask for something, so he went to her house and asked her about her needs, so Imām 'Alī ﵇ told the Messenger of God ﷺ about the severe harm and agony that had befallen her.

He ﷺ said, "I will teach you that which is more useful to you than a servant. When you go to sleep, glorify God thirty three times, give praise to Him thirty three times and say *Takbīr* (God is Great) thirty four times."

He said: Then Fatima raised her head and said three times, "I am content with God and His Messenger."[91]

That father who was capable of filling his daughter's house with gold, silver, slaves and bondmaids, and who never rejected anyone who asked him for a favor except that he had fulfilled that favor for him, refrained from providing a

---

[91] Ṣadūq, Shaykh Muḥammad b. 'Alī, *'Ilal al-Sharāi'*, Vol. 2, p. 366, ch. 88, *'Illat Tasbīḥ Fāṭimah;* Ṣadūq, Shaykh Muḥammad b. 'Alī, *Man Lā Yaḥḍuruh al-Faqīh*, Vol. 1, p. 211; Ṭabrisī, Shaykh Faḍl b. Ḥasan, *Makārim al-Akhlāq*, p. 280; Ibn al-Maghāzlī, *Manāqīb al-Imām 'Alī b. Abī Tālib*, Vol. 3, p. 341; and other specialized references.

Thakha'ir al-'Uqba, p. 49; *Musnad Aḥmad b. Ḥanbal*, Vol. 1, p. 80, 96, 106, 136, 146, 153; Bukhārī, Muḥammad b. Ismā'īl, *Ṣaḥīḥ Bukhārī*, Vol. 4, p. 48 and Vol. 6, p. 193, ch. *al-Nafaqāt, Khādim al-Mar'a*, and Vol. 7, p. 149, ch. *al-Da'awāt, al-Takbīr wal-Tasbīḥ 'Ind al-Manām*; Muslim b. al-Ḥajjāj, *Ṣaḥīḥ Muslim*, Vol. 8, p. 84; al-Sijistānī, Abū Dāwūd, *Sunan Abī Dāwūd*, Vol. 30, p. 489; al-Ḥakim al-Nīshāpūrī, *al-Mustadrak 'ala al-Ṣaḥīḥayn*, Vol. 3, p. 152; al-Bayhaqī, *Sunan al-Kubra lil Bayhaqī*, Vol. 7, p. 293; 'Alī al-Haythamī, *Majma' al-Zawā'id*, Vol. 10, p. 100; *Musnad Abī Ya'la*, Vol. 1, p. 419; al-Ḥanafī, Muḥammad b. Yūsuf al-Zarandī, *Naẓm Durar al-Simṭayn*, p. 189; Yūsuf b. al-Zakī al-Mizzī, *Tahdhīb al-Kamāl fī Asmā' al-Rijāl*, Vol. 21, p. 253; al-Ṭayālisī, Abū Dāwūd Sulaymān b. Dāwūd, *Musnad Abī Dawūd al-Ṭayālīsī*, p. 16; and other general references.

servant to the leader of all women who was a part of the Prophet ﷺ and whose worry and annoyance cause him worry and annoyance as well.[92]

He refrained from fulfilling this urgent need for his daughter who is the most beloved person to his heart, out of pure altruism whereby he favored the poor people of his nation over his own heart.

This was the practice of the one who was sent by God for the purpose of nurturing his nation, as per God's ﷻ saying:

---

[92] *Faḍā'il al-Ṣaḥābah*, p. 78.

Musnad Aḥmad b. Ḥanbal, Vol. 4, p 328.

Bukhārī, Muḥammad b. Ismā'īl, *Ṣaḥīḥ Bukhārī*, Vol. 6, p. 158.

﴿وَيُؤْثِرُونَ عَلَىٰ أَنْفُسِهِمْ وَلَوْ كَانَ بِهِمْ خَصَاصَةٌ﴾

﴾*wa-yu'thirūna 'alā 'anfusihim*
wa-law kāna bihim khaṣāṣatun﴿

﴾*but prefer [the Immigrants] to themselves, though*
poverty be their own lot﴿[93]

---

[93] Sūrat al-Ḥashr, Verse 9.

Examples from His Interactions and Morals

He ﷺ used to sit on the ground.[94]

He used to eat with the slaves and salute the young boys.[95]

He used to eat what the slave ate, and sit like the slave sat.[96]

Once, a Bedouin woman passed by him and he was sitting and eating on the ground. So, she said, "O' Muḥammad, by God, you are but eating the food of slaves and sitting like them." Then, the Messenger of God ﷺ said to her, "Watch your words! Which servant is more obedient to God than me?"[97]

---

[94] Ṭūsī, Shaykh Muḥammad b. Ḥasan, *al-Amālī*, p. 393.

[95] Ṣadūq, Shaykh Muḥammad b. ʿAlī, *al-Amālī*, al-Majlis 17, ḥadīth 2, p. 130.

[96] al-Barqī, Aḥmad b. Muḥammad b. Khālid, *al-Maḥāsin*, p. 456, ch. 51, ḥadīth 386.

[97] al-Barqī, Aḥmad b. Muḥammad b. Khālid, *al-Maḥāsin*, p. 457, ḥadīth 388.

Kulaynī, Shaykh Muḥammad b. Yaʿqūb, *al-Kāfī*, Vol. 2, p. 157.

He used to patch his clothes.[98]

He used to milk his parents' goats, respond to the requests of the free man and the slave.[99]

He used to visit the ill in the farthest areas of the city.[100]

He used to sit with the poor and eat with the vulnerable.[101]

When someone would shake his hand, the Prophet ﷺ would not let go of his hand until that person removed his hand first.[102]

He used to sit wherever the gathering allowed him to sit.[103]

---

[98] Ibn al-Maghāzlī, *Manāqīb al-Imām 'Alī b. Abī Tālib*, Vol. 1, p. 146.

[99] Ibid.

[100] Ibid.

[101] Ibid.

[102] Ibid, p. 147.

[103] Ibid, p. 146.

He would not gaze at length into people's faces.[104]

He would be angry for his Lord – never for himself.[105]

A man came to speak to him, yet he was intimated of him. So, the Prophet ﷺ told him, "Take it easy, I am not a king. Rather, I am the son of a woman who used to eat old and preserved meat."[106]

His servant, ʾAnas b. Mālik said, "I served the Prophet ﷺ for nine years during which he never asked me to do anything nor criticized me."[107]

One day, while he ﷺ was sitting in the mosque, a bondmaid came to some of the companions while he was present. She touched the end of his garment, so the Prophet ﷺ stood up for her. However, she did not say a word. And the

---

104 Ibid.

105 Ibid.

106 Ṭabrisī, Shaykh Faḍl b. Ḥasan, *Makārim al-Akhlāq*, p. 16.

107 Ibid.

Prophet ﷺ did not address her either. She, then, repeated what she did three times. So, the Prophet ﷺ stood up for her as she was standing behind him. So, she took a fringe of his clothes and left.

People said to her, "You restrained the Messenger of God ﷺ three times, whereby neither you nor he said any word to the other! What did you want from him?!"

She said, "We have an ill person at home; and my parents sent me to take a fringe of the Prophet's ﷺ clothes by which he would be cured. When I intended to take it, he saw me and stood up. So, I felt shy to take it while he was looking at me, and I didn't want to take permission from him to take it. So, I took it."[108]

This incident indicates his deep care for the dignity of a human being; for, he ﷺ was aware of the bondmaid's wish yet he didn't ask her to spare her the humiliation of making such a request. To what extent does a person cherish the value and dignity of man, if he is this keen to

---

[108] Kulaynī, Shaykh Muḥammad b. Yaʿqūb, *al-Kāfī*, Vol. 2, p. 102.

preserve the dignity of a bondmaid with such manners and cautiousness?!

During the time when the Jews lived in his ﷺ country, and dealt with others on the basis of trust and oaths, he was in the most powerful position. The Messenger of God ﷺ owed one of these Jews a few Dinars; therefore, the man filed a lawsuit against the Prophet ﷺ. So, he ﷺ told him, "I don't have anything to give you." He said, "I won't leave you alone, O' Muḥammad, until you pay me back." So, he said, "Then, I will sit with you." He then sat with him until he prayed – in that place – the Noon, Afternoon, Sunset, Dinner and Dawn prayers!

The Prophet's ﷺ companions would threaten him, so the Messenger of God ﷺ looked at them and said: "What are you doing to him?" They said: "Is it acceptable for a Jew to detain you?"

He ﷺ said, "God did not send me to oppress someone with whom we have made an oath – nor anyone else."

During mid-day, the Jewish man said, "I bear witness that there is no God but God and that Muḥammad is his servant and Messenger, and that my money is to be given for the sake of God. By God, all that I have done was to verify your attributes that were mentioned in the Torah. For, I have read in the Torah that: Muḥammad b. 'Abdillāh will be born in Makkah and will immigrate to Tayba. He is not rude nor mean nor does he raise his voice. He does not use obscene language. And I bear witness that there is no God but Him, and that you are the Messenger of God. Behold my money, you may use it in whichever way God wants – provided that the Jewish man was quite wealthy.".[109]

It was narrated that 'Aqba b. 'Alqama said, "I came to 'Alī while he was holding horribly sour yogurt and a dry piece of bread. So, I said: "O' 'Amīr al-Mu'minīn, is this what you eat?" He said: "O' Abā al-Junūd, I saw the Messenger of God eating food dryer than this piece of bread. Therefore, I fear that if I don't follow in the

---

[109] Ṣadūq, Shaykh Muḥammad b. 'Alī, *al-Amālī*, al-Majlis 71, ḥadīth 6, p. 552.

Messenger of God's footsteps, I might not be with him."[110]

Someone asked Imām Zayn al-'Ābidīn, 'Alī b. al-Ḥusayn ﷺ – who was known for his ideal worship, "How close is your worship to the worship of your grandfather?" He said, "My worship is to my grandfather's worship as my grandfather's worship is to the worship of the Messenger of God."[111]

During the last days of his life, he pardoned his murderer,[112] by which he demonstrated the proximity of his virtuousness to the Beneficent attributes of God ﷻ:

---

[110] Ṭabrisī, Shaykh Faḍl b. Ḥasan, *Makārim al-Akhlāq*, p. 158.

Ibn Abi l-Ḥadīd, *Sharḥ Nahj al-Balāgha* Vol. 2, p. 201.

[111] Ibn Abi l-Ḥadīd, *Sharḥ Nahj al-Balāgha*, Vol. 1, p. 27,.

Majlisī, 'Allamah Muḥammad Bāqir, *Biḥār al-Anwār*, Vol. 41, p. 149.

[112] Kulaynī, Shaykh Muḥammad b. Ya'qūb, *al-Kāfī*, Vol. 2, p. 108, ch. *'Imān and Kufr*, ch. *al-'Afu*, ḥadīth 9.

﴿وَمَا أَرْسَلْنَاكَ إِلَّا رَحْمَةً لِلْعَالَمِينَ﴾

﴿*wa-mā ʾarsalnāka ʾillā raḥmatan li-l-ʿālamīn* [a]﴾

﴿*We did not send* you *but*
as a mercy to all the nations.[*]﴾[113]

Only the likes of this Great Prophet ﷺ can say: "Indeed, I have been sent to perfect the good virtues."[114]

How can one explain the virtues of the one who God ﷻ addresses when He ﷻ said:

﴿وَإِنَّكَ لَعَلَىٰ خُلُقٍ عَظِيمٍ﴾

﴿*wa-ʾinnaka la-ʿalā khuluqin ʿaẓīm* [in]﴾

﴿*And indeed, you possess a great character*﴾[115]

---

[113] Sūrat al-Anbiyāʾ, Verse 107.

[*] Or 'to all the worlds.'

[114] Jamʿ al-Bayān, Vol. 10, p. 86.

[115] Sūrat al-Qalam, Verse 4.

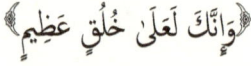

A brief overview of his life, virtues and attributes is sufficient to make a fair man believe in his prophethood:

﴿يَا أَيُّهَا النَّبِيُّ إِنَّا أَرْسَلْنَاكَ شَاهِدًا وَمُبَشِّرًا وَنَذِيرًا﴾

﴿yā-'ayyuhā n-nabiyyu 'innā 'arsalnāka shāhidan wa-mubashshiran wa-nadhīra [n]﴾

﴿وَدَاعِيًا إِلَى اللَّهِ بِإِذْنِهِ وَسِرَاجًا مُنِيرًا﴾

﴿wa-dā'iyan 'ilā llāhi bi-'idhnihī wa-sirājan munīra [n]﴾

﴿*O' Prophet! Indeed We have sent* you *as a witness, as a bearer of good news and as a warner and as a summoner to God by His permission, and as a radiant lamp*﴾[116]

---

[116] Sūrat al-Aḥzāb, Verses 45-46.

www.ingramcontent.com/pod-product-compliance
Lightning Source LLC
Chambersburg PA
CBHW031442120626
46545CB00006B/2522
* 9 7 8 1 9 5 6 2 7 6 2 9 9 *